POLITICAL SCIENCE
for Kids

Presidential vs Parliamentary Systems of Government

Politics for Kids

6th Grade Social Studies

BABY PROFESSOR

EDUCATION KIDS

Speedy Publishing LLC

40 E. Main St. #1156

Newark, DE 19711

www.speedypublishing.com

Copyright 2018

In this book, we're going to talk about the presidential versus the parliamentary systems of government. So, let's get right to it!

AGREEMENT

ELECTION PROGRAM

POLITICS

SPEECH

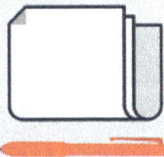

DECREE

VOTE

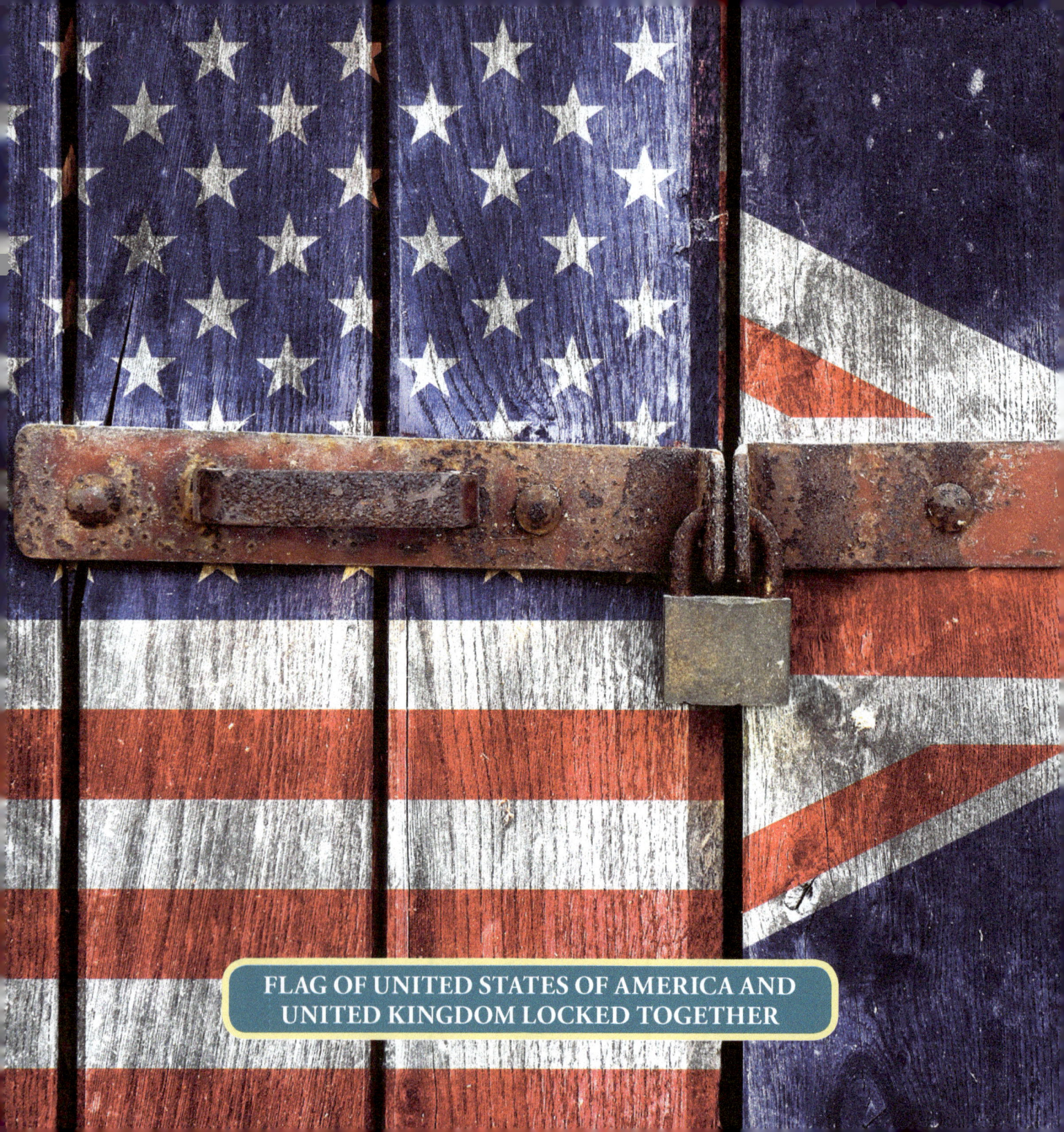
FLAG OF UNITED STATES OF AMERICA AND
UNITED KINGDOM LOCKED TOGETHER

MODELS OF DEMOCRATIC GOVERNMENTS

Democratic governments are run with two different models. For example, the United States is a democracy that uses a presidential model. On the other hand, the United Kingdom, which is also a democracy, uses a parliamentary model.

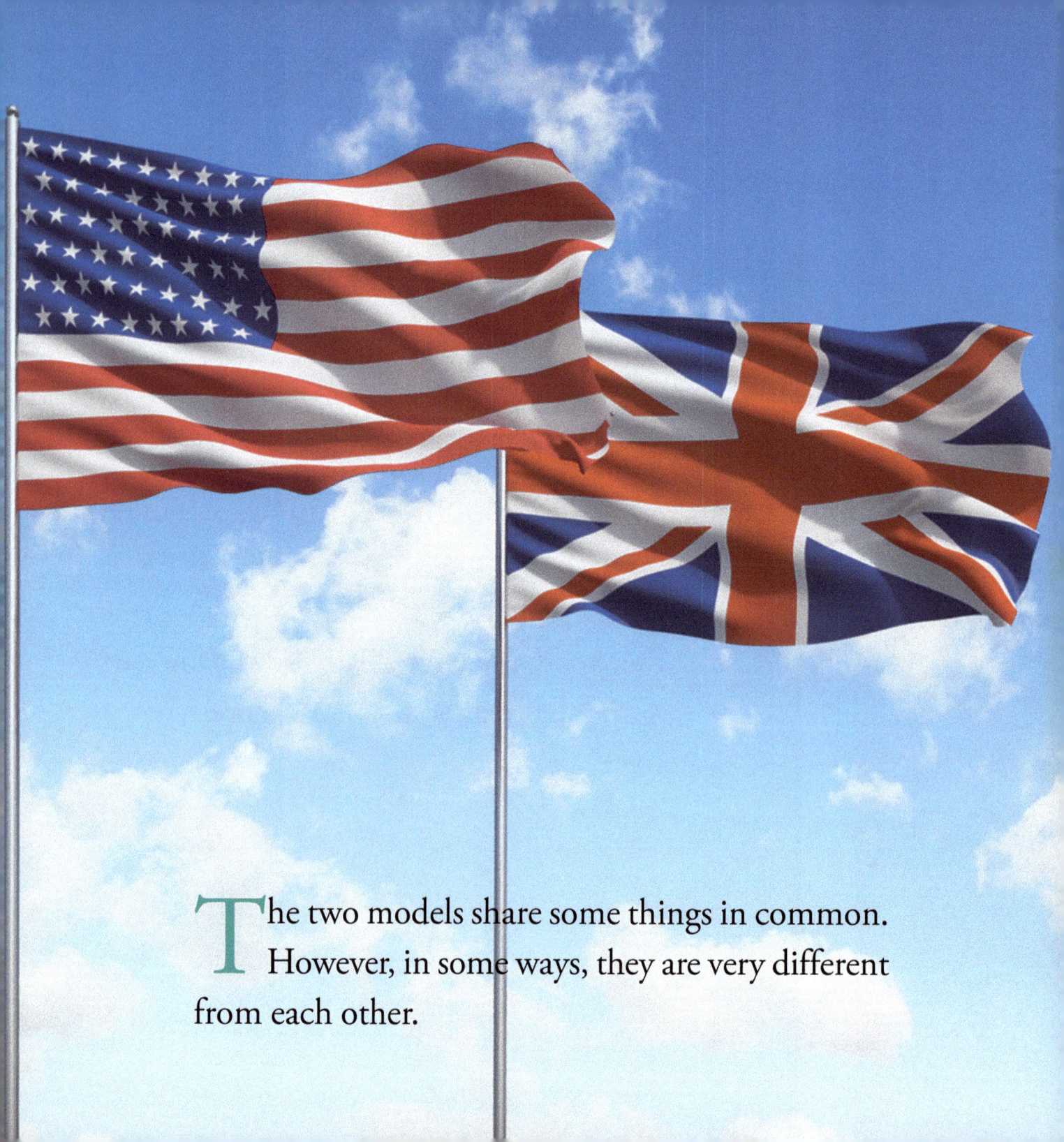

The two models share some things in common. However, in some ways, they are very different from each other.

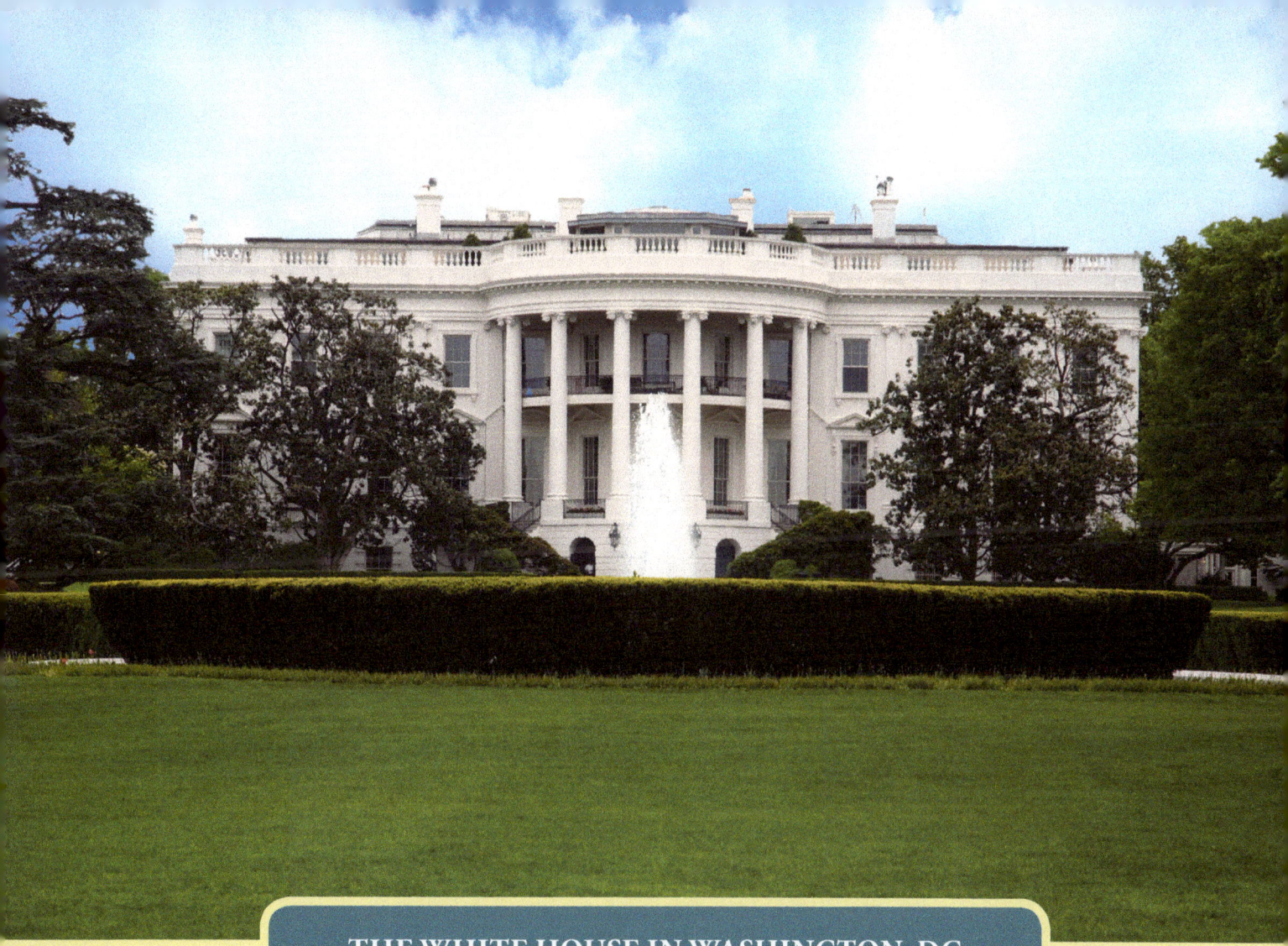

THE WHITE HOUSE IN WASHINGTON, DC

Not all democratic governments have a purely presidential or purely parliamentary model. Instead, some governments operate with a system that is a blend of both.

For example, the United States has a full presidential system, but the government of South Africa has a system that is semi-presidential and France's government has a presidency that is connected to a parliament.

One thing that is common to all democratic governments is that the citizens have a hand in governing the country. The citizens either manage the government themselves or, as is more common, it's managed through representatives.

HAND CASTING A VOTE

These representatives hold their positions because they were elected by the people. Authoritarian governments place limits on the amount of participation their citizens have in the government. Some governments don't allow their citizens to participate at all!

THE PRESIDENTIAL SYSTEM

The presidential system of government has an executive branch that exists separately from the legislature. In a presidential system, the President has a major role to play. He or she is the head of state in addition to being the chief executive.

PRESIDENT OF CHINA XI JINPING AND PRESIDENT OF KAZAKHSTAN NURSULTAN NAZARBAYEV

The President is elected in a process that is completely separate from how the members of the legislature are elected. The President's powers are balanced and limited by the powers that the legislature has.

The President doesn't write up or offer bills for review. The legislature is in charge of creating bills. Then, they debate and decide on whether to pass the bills that are proposed. When a bill is up for adoption, before it becomes part of the "law of the land," the President may decide to veto it, which means that he or she doesn't approve it.

PRESIDENT REAGAN SPEAKING
IN MINNEAPOLIS 1982

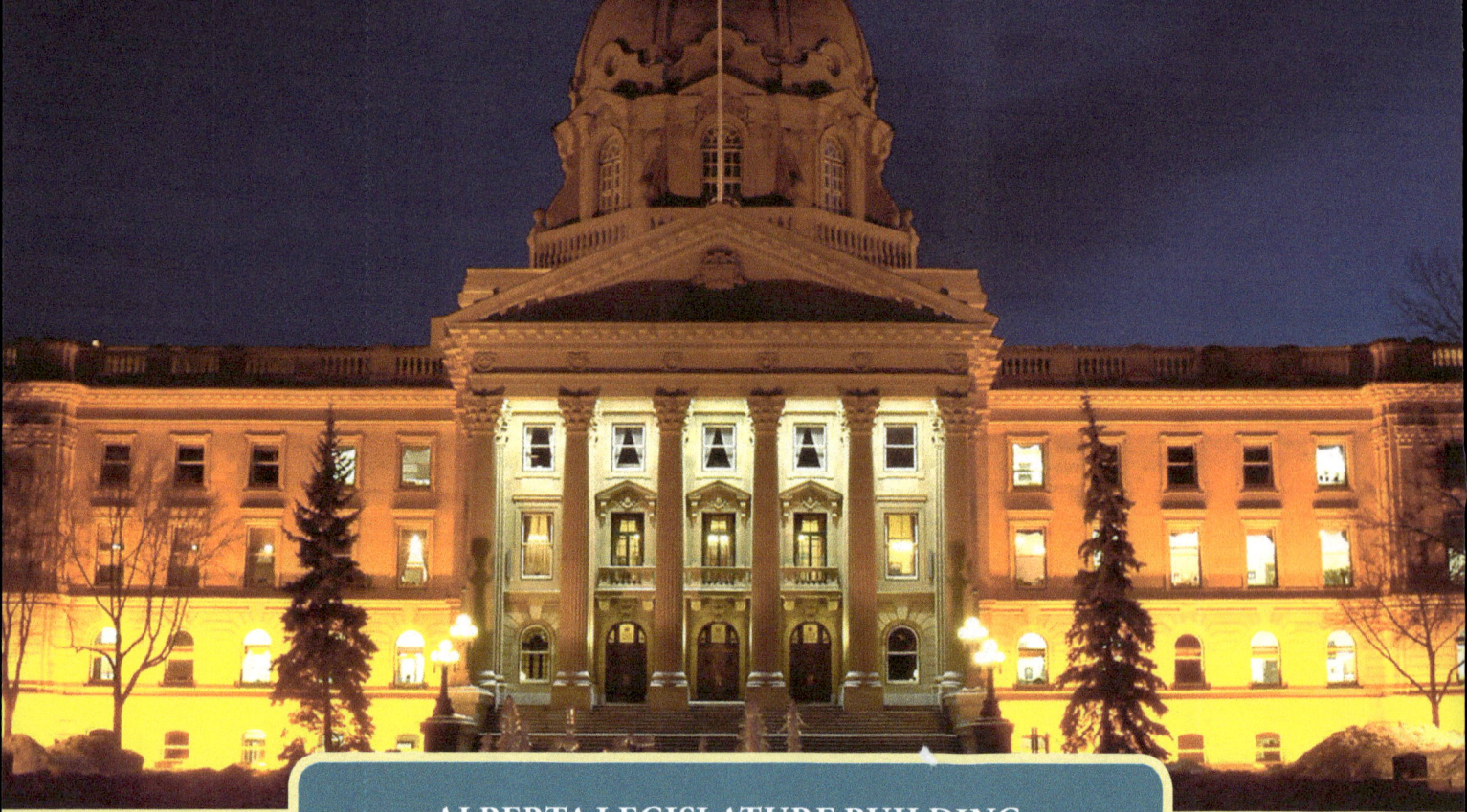

ALBERTA LEGISLATURE BUILDING

The members of the legislature have the power to negate the President's veto if they can gather enough votes to do so.

CORONATION OF BRITISH MONARCH GEORGE VI IN 1937

This practice of a President either approving, disapproving, or just letting a bill pass without a response comes from the tradition in Great Britain. The British monarch had to approve the acts proposed by Parliament.

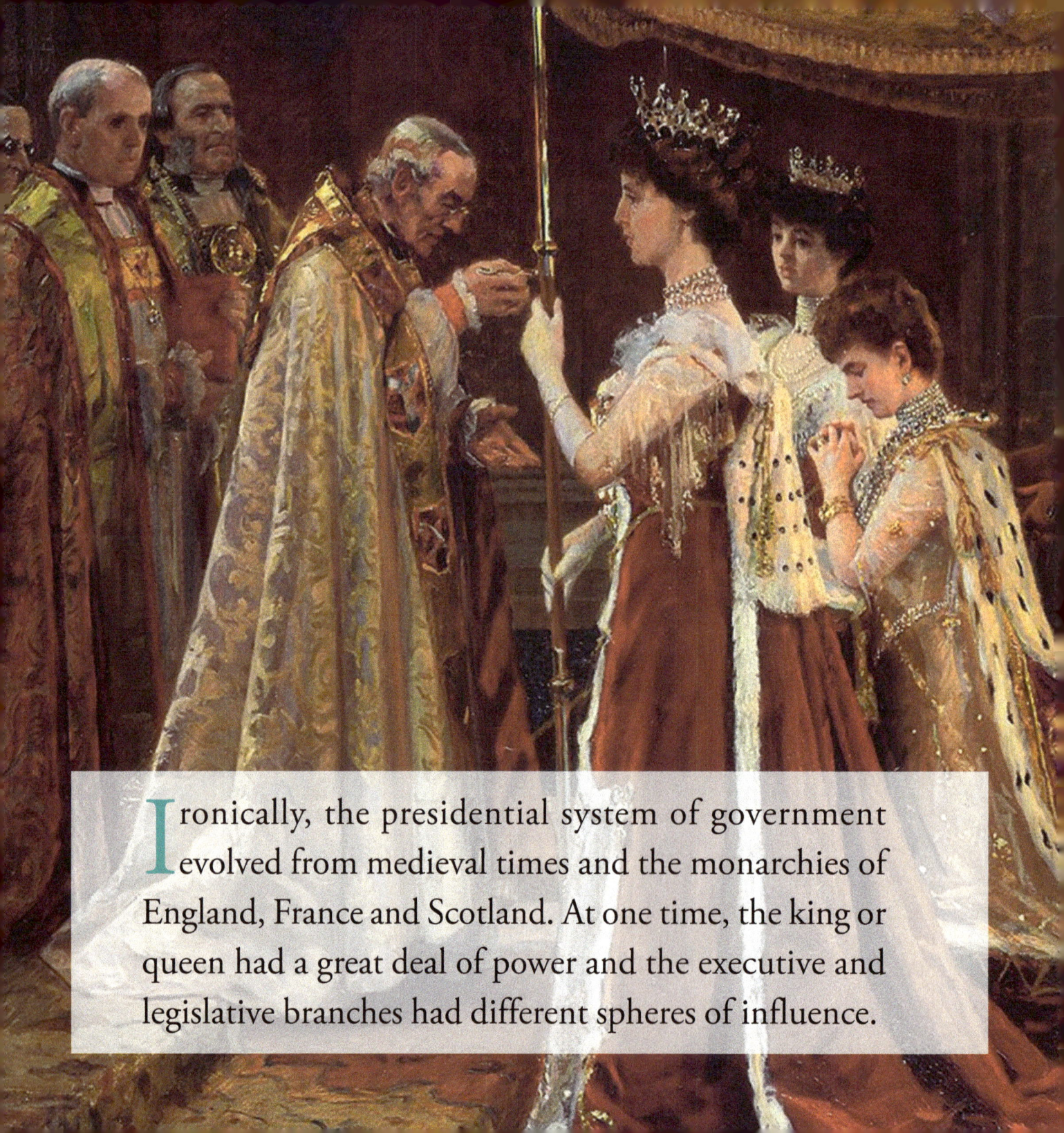

Ironically, the presidential system of government evolved from medieval times and the monarchies of England, France and Scotland. At one time, the king or queen had a great deal of power and the executive and legislative branches had different spheres of influence.

THE ANOINTING OF QUEEN ALEXANDRA

ELIZABETH I OF ENGLAND

However, the role of the king or queen diminished over time in these countries, whereas the power of the United States President increased. Those who criticize the United States government say that the president has too much power and that there really isn't a distinct separation between the three different branches of government.

One of the areas where the President has a great deal of power is in foreign affairs. The President can make decisions regarding military deployment, but doesn't have the right to declare a state of war with another nation without the approval of Congress.

PRESIDENT ABRAHAM LINCOLN
16TH PRESIDENT OF THE UNITED STATES

There are many ways that a President's power is kept in check. One of the ways is that a president has a fixed term in the position. Elections are events that are scheduled every four years.

PRESIDENTIAL ELECTION CANDIDATES ENGAGED IN POLITICAL DEBATES IN FRONT OF POTENTIAL VOTERS

They can't be triggered by a procedure of Parliament or other action. The exception to this rule, only available in certain countries, is when a president is thought to have committed an illegal act.

THE PARLIAMENTARY SYSTEM

The word "parliamentary" comes from the word "parley," which means a discussion. King Henry III and his nobles, who were members of the Great Council, discussed the country in the 13th century and made decisions.

ANNO · ETATIS ·   · SVÆ · XLIX ·

HENRY VIII OF ENGLAND

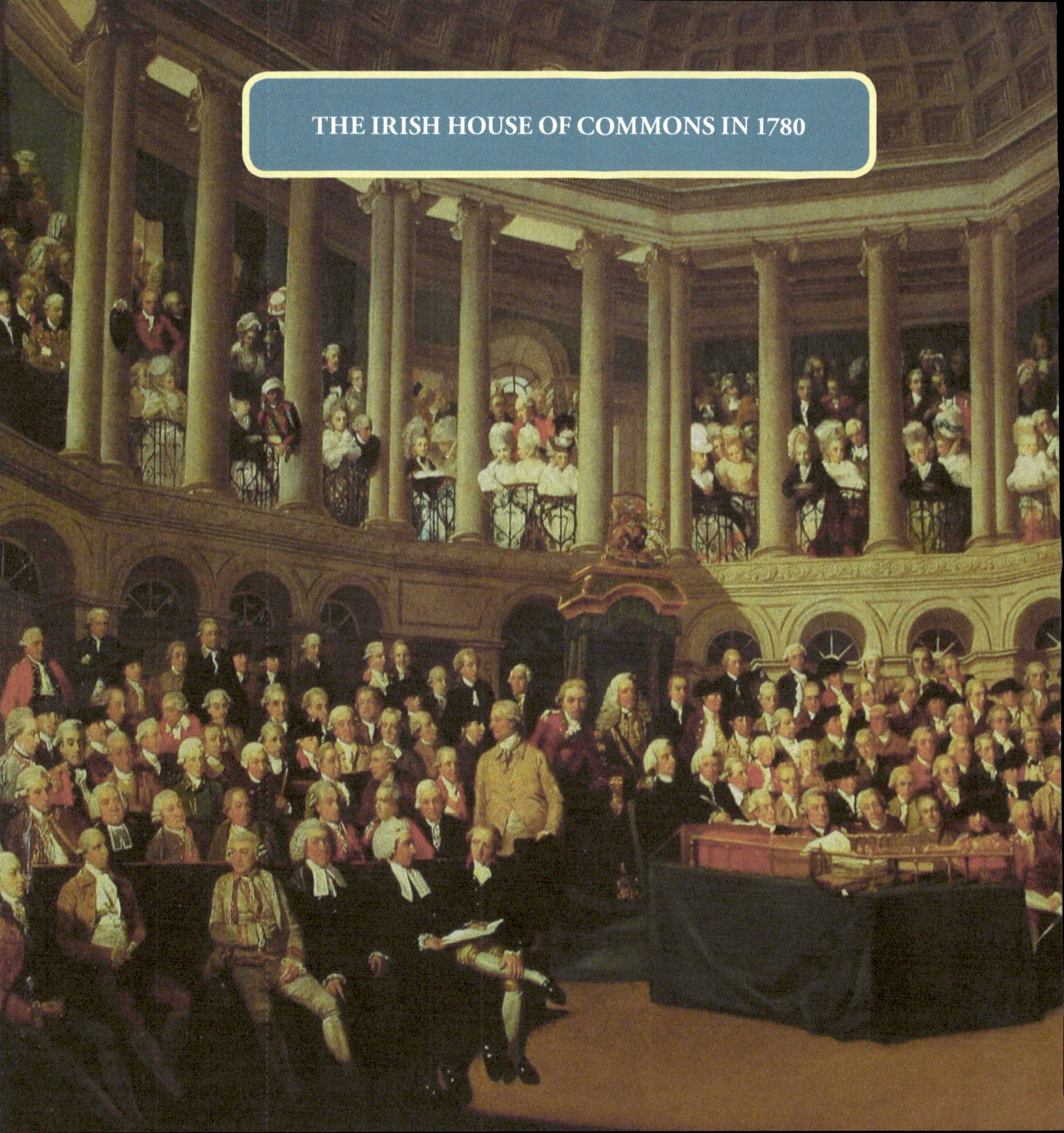

THE IRISH HOUSE OF COMMONS IN 1780

Eventually, the Great Council became known as the "House of Lords." Representatives from the counties and the villages within those counties became known as the "House of Commons." Today there are three divisions of Parliament including these two houses and the monarch who is the king or queen.

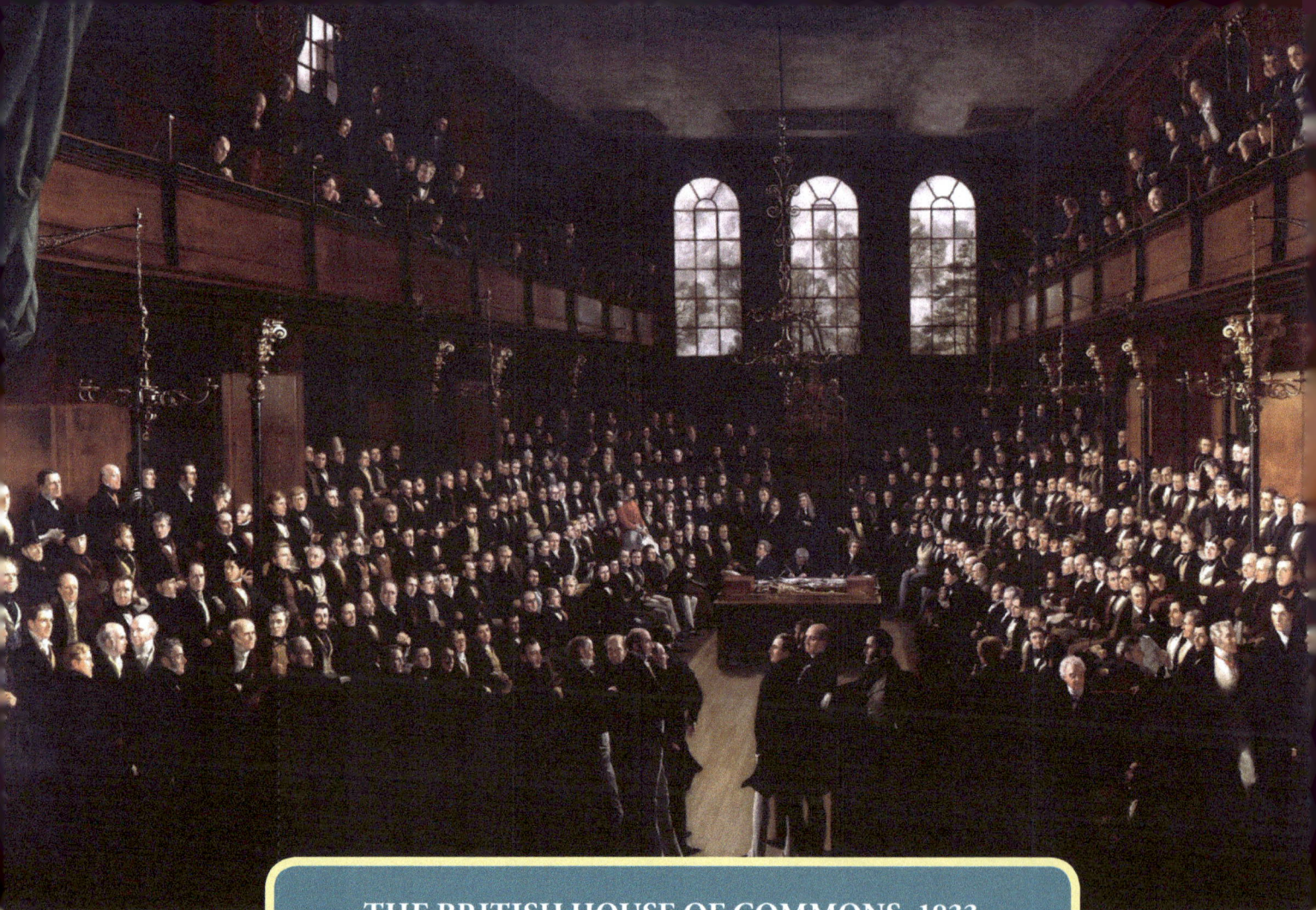

THE BRITISH HOUSE OF COMMONS, 1833

In the United Kingdom, the members of the House of Commons are elected by the population in England as well as by votes from those living in Wales, Scotland, and the northern section of Ireland. For many centuries, these

Members of Parliament, called MPs for short, weren't given a salary, but since the 20th century they have been paid.

PASOK MPS IN THE GREEK PARLIAMENT DURING 2009 BUDGET DISCUSSION

Elections for MPs are held on a regular basis every five years. The House of Lords members are NOT elected, but instead have inherited their seats or are appointed by the Prime Minister. The House of Lords members have responsibilities that relate to three main functions. One of their functions is to challenge what the government does. Along with the House of Commons, their second function is to shape new laws.

QUEEN ANNE IN THE HOUSE OF LORDS
CIRCA 1708-1714

HOUSE OF LORDS CHAMBER

Their third function is to investigate issues through the use of debates and committees in order to improve the way the government is run. Because the members of the House of Lords are not elected, there has been a great deal of debate about eventually abolishing them despite their long history.

In a parliamentary system, the functions of the head of state and the chief executive are not handled by the same individual. Parliamentary systems make a clear distinction between these two roles. The head of the government is typically a premier or the prime minister.

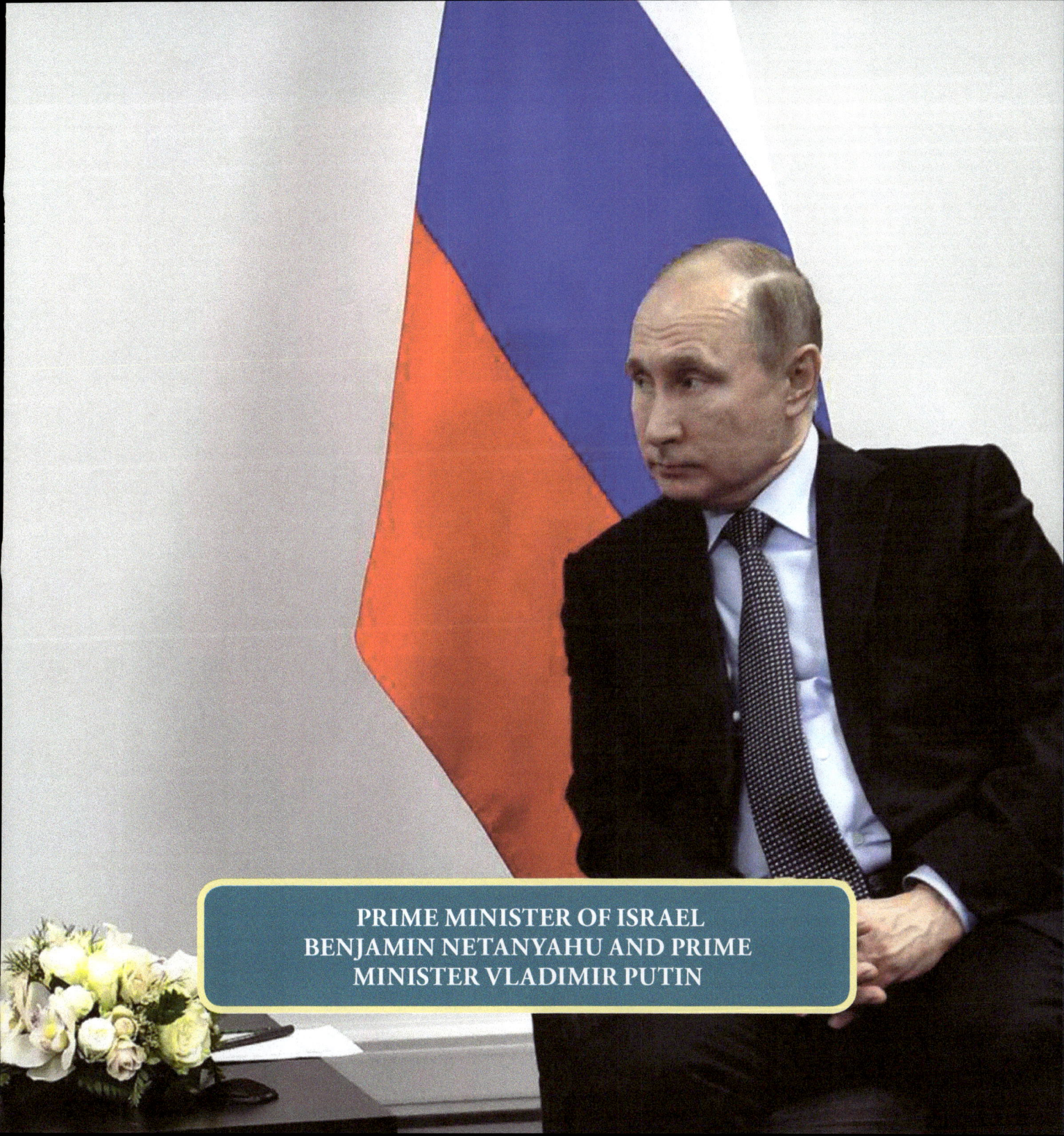

PRIME MINISTER OF ISRAEL
BENJAMIN NETANYAHU AND PRIME
MINISTER VLADIMIR PUTIN

The head of state is either a hereditary king or queen or a president who has been elected either by the parliament or through a popular vote. Most countries of Europe have retained a parliamentary system, with the government of Great Britain as the most commonly known. At one time in history, Great Britain was a monarchy and was ruled by a king or queen, but over time the monarchy lost power.

QUEEN VICTORIA

CANADIAN PRIME MINISTER JUSTIN TRUDEAU

Now the monarchy functions as the head of state and the role of chief executive is the role fulfilled by the position of Prime Minister. Many countries that formerly belonged to Great Britain don't have royal families so they consider the queen of England their figurehead. This is true of Canada, Australia and New Zealand.

COMPARING THE TWO SYSTEMS

Here are some of the main differences and main commonalities of these two types of democratic systems.

The way the chief executive is elected is different depending on whether the government is presidential or parliamentary. In the United States, the President is elected by a combination of the popular vote and the votes of the Electoral College.

In parliamentary systems, the legislature chooses the chief executive, who is the Prime Minister. Because there is a blending of executive and legislative in parliamentary systems, members of a particular party almost always vote along party lines.

This is less true in presidential systems where legislators don't always have to fall into alignment with their own party, but are more free to choose what they feel is best.

The style of debate is very different between the two systems. In the presidential system, members have the right to keep their speeches going in order to delay the legislators from taking action. This is called a filibuster. On the other hand, in parliamentary systems, the members may call for the debate on a particular topic to end so the vote can begin. This action is called cloture.

PEOPLE'S FILIBUSTER NEW YORK CITY

MEMBER OF ROMANIAN PARLIAMENT
IS VOTING BY RAISING HIS HAND

Both systems can oust their chief executive if there is a reason for doing so, but the way the process is carried out is different depending on the system. In presidential systems, the members of Congress can follow a process to impeach the President. In parliamentary systems, if the majority of the Parliament vote to do so, they can take their Prime Minister out of office.

In a pure presidential system, such as the system in the United States, the President is both the head of state as well as the chief executive.

In Great Britain, the king or queen is the head of state and the chief executive is the Prime Minister.

THE FUTURE OF DEMOCRACY

Since the Soviet Union fell, there has been an increase in democracy around the world. Many emerging nations are considering whether they want a more traditional parliamentary system or a more flexible presidential style of government. They can also create a unique hybrid of both systems. The United States has a full presidential system. There are some aspects of it that many people believe should be revised.

SUMMARY

Democracy is growing throughout the world. Many nations are actively considering whether they want to institute a presidential or parliamentary system of government. These are the two major models, but some countries are creating models that are hybrids of both systems.

Now that you've read about the presidential versus the parliamentary systems of government, you may want to read about jury duty in the Baby Professor book

Jury Duty - US Government and Politics | Children's Government Books.

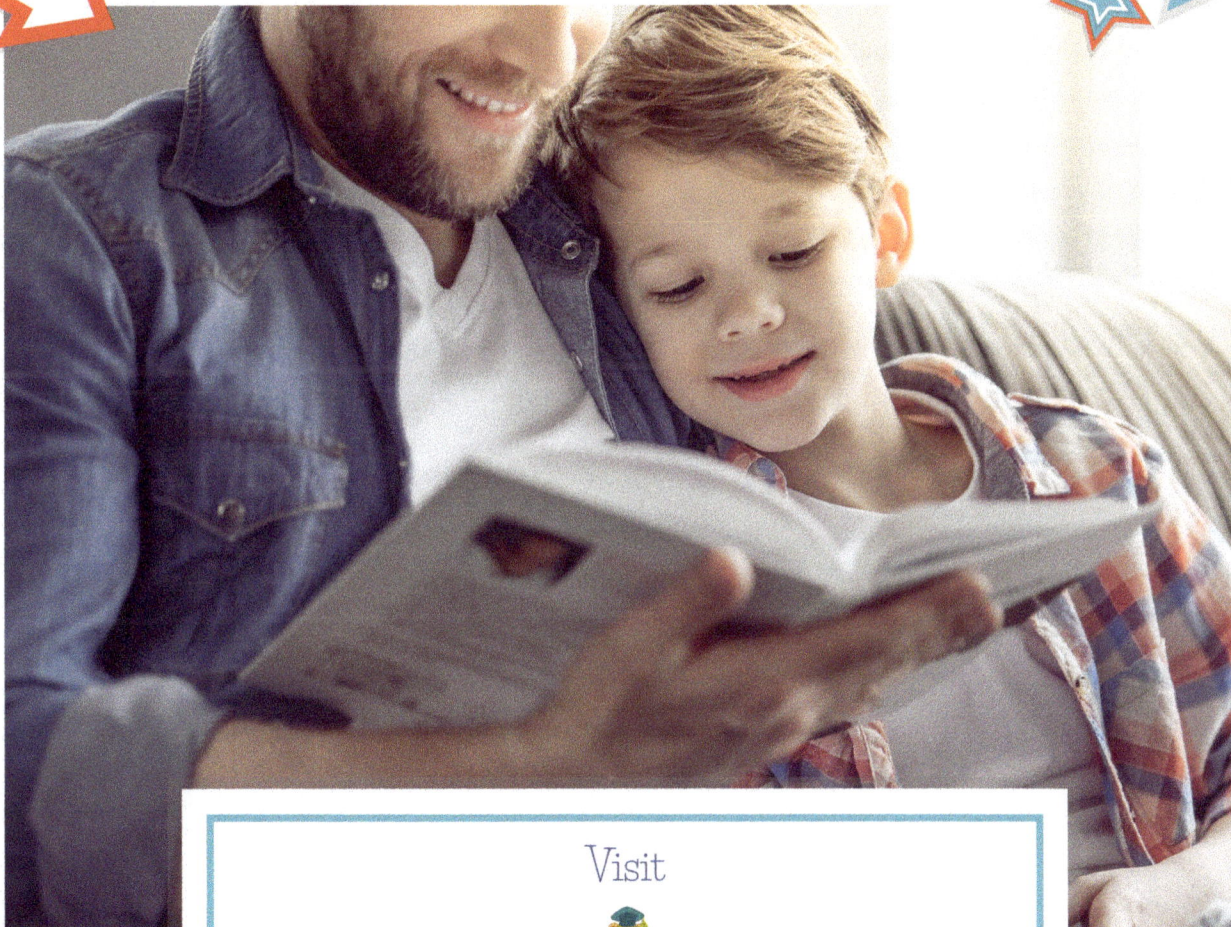

Visit

BABY PROFESSOR
EDUCATION KIDS

www.BabyProfessorBooks.com

to download Free Baby Professor eBooks and view
our catalog of new and exciting Children's Books

Milton Keynes UK
Ingram Content Group UK Ltd.
UKHW050449060924
447585UK00027B/99

9 798869 414663